1. The 'L' Class destroyer *Lively* was laid down on 20 December 1938 and completed by Cammell Laird on 20 July 1941. She served with Force 'H' until October 1941, when she was transferred to Force 'K' (Malta). She took part in the destruction of two Italian convoys off Spartivento on the night of 18 November 1941 and saw action with Italian heavy units off Sirte, sustaining 15in shell damage from the battleship *Littorio*. She suffered two direct bomb hits off Crete on 13 May 1942, and capsized and sank in four minutes. The photograph shows *Lively* at speed in 1941–42.

⚓ **WARSHIPS ILLUSTRATED No 4**

BRITISH DESTROYERS
in World War Two

R. A. BURT

ARMS AND ARMOUR PRESS

Introduction

Published in 1985 by Arms and Armour Press,
2–6 Hampstead High Street, London NW3 1QQ.

Distributed in the United States by
Sterling Publishing Co. Inc., 2 Park Avenue,
New York, N.Y. 10016.

British Library Cataloguing in Publication Data:
Burt, R. A.
British destroyers in World War Two. – (Warships
illustrated; 4)
1. Great Britain. *Royal Navy* 2. Destroyers
(Warships) – Great Britain – History 3. World
War, 1939–1945 – Naval operations, British
I. Title   II. Series
623.8′254′0941   V825.5.G7
ISBN 0-85368-748-X

Editing, design and artwork by Roger Chesneau.
Typesetting by Typesetters (Birmingham) Ltd.
Printed in Italy by Tipolitografia G. Canale
& C. S.p.A., Turin, in association with Keats
European Ltd.

The huge construction programmes sanctioned by Parliament during the First World War gave Great Britain one of the largest destroyer fleets in the world, but after the war vast numbers of this type were surplus to requirements, and many of the older and smaller vessels were either laid up or scrapped. Moreover, during the interwar years – despite the experience gained in 1914–18, which showed the need for adequate numbers of these ships for escort protection and anti-submarine work – construction of new destroyers was reduced considerably, both because of the desire to abide by the Washington and London Naval Treaties and as a result of the assumption that no major war would take place in the next twenty-five years.

In 1939 Britain entered the Second World War with just ninety modern destroyers and the rest, having been constructed between 1918 and 1920, virtually obsolete. Nevertheless, these older vessels constituted the backbone of the destroyer force, and all rendered sterling service throughout the hostilities, many of them being modernized in varying degrees to suit specialized roles, for example as anti-submarine or anti-aircraft escorts. Emergency construction programmes were soon under way, but it was in the early stages of the war, when Britain stood alone, that the need for destroyers was greatest, especially as the type suffered heavy losses during the first two years of the conflict.

Destroyers saw more action than any other type of warship, and were involved in practically every sea battle across the globe: no other warship type suffered heavier casualties in the First World War, and history would repeat itself in the Second. Names such as *Ashanti*, *Kelly*, *Kipling*, *Laforey*, *Cossack*, *Hardy*, *Saumarez* and *Glowworm* blazed their way into the history books, performing deeds far beyond the call of duty.

Destroyers, as we knew them forty years ago, are now extinct, their role taken over by the modern guided missile frigate of today, but it is doubtful whether any other type of vessel can emulate their legendary exploits or hold the special appeal they had for the men who served in them.

The photographs used in this volume are all from the impressive wartime collections of the Admiralty and Ministry of Defence, which are now housed at the Imperial War Museum, and my sincere thanks are extended to that establishment for permission to use them. Grateful thanks are also due to A. S. Norris who gave both assistance and material during the preparation of the book.

Ray Burt

◄2
2. *Martin* early in 1942. She was one of the 'M' Class lost on 10 November that year. See also photograph 63.

▲3 ▼4

6

3. *Skate* was one of the oldest destroyers to serve with the Royal Navy during the Second World War. Launched in January 1917 as a unit of the Admiralty-designed 'R' Class and then later fitted out as a minelayer, she was further altered in 1940 to become a magnetic minesweeper and then once more for escort duties in 1942; after a prolonged and extremely active life, she was scrapped in 1947. The photograph shows her as an escort destroyer during early 1943: note her forecastle and midships 4in Mk. IV guns trained to starboard, 44in searchlight, the depth charges at the stern, and the 0.5in AA guns between the second and third funnels.

4. The original design for *Wallace* was proposed by Thornycroft in 1916, and accepted within a few months after slight modifications to suit the Board's requirements. She was completed in 1919 and is seen here in her role of escort destroyer after conversion in 1939 when she had twin 4in Mk. XIX fitted in 'B' and 'X' positions, replacing 4.7in Mk. Is. Painted in her Admiralty Disruptive

camouflage, she shows all the usual wartime modifications applicable to destroyers, including radar on the lattice mast behind the second funnel, on the director over the bridge and on the masthead – which incorporated aerials for Talk Between Ships (TBS) and Identification Friend or Foe (IFF).

5. A sister ship to *Wallace*, and another unit of the Thorneycroft-designed *Shakespeare* Class, *Broke* (ex-*Rooke*, renamed shortly after completion) was commissioned in 1920 and was thus almost twenty years old at the outbreak of the Second World War. Nevertheless, she performed sterling service during the first three years of the war, before she was unfortunately sunk by gunfire from shore batteries off Algiers in November 1942. Note that in this photograph *Broke*, unlike *Wallace*, retains the original 4.7in guns and that her Type 272 warning radar has been fitted over the bridge. The photograph was taken on 18 July 1942.

5 ▼

 ▲6 ▼7

8▲

9▲

6. Although another unit of the *Shakespeare* Class, *Keppel* was not completed until 1925, having been laid up at Portsmouth in 1921 pending further investigations into destroyer requirements by the Board of Admiralty. The ship is seen here in March 1943 whilst in Portsmouth Dockyard. Note the high-frequency/medium-frequency (HF/MF) direction finder aerials on the mainmast. *Keppel* was scrapped postwar.

7. *Douglas* was one of eight *Scott* Class destroyers built to an Admiralty design by Cammell Laird in Birkenhead (six units) and Hawthorn Leslie (two). Completed in August 1918, *Douglas* continued in her destroyer role until 1939 when she was converted into a long-range escort ship. The photograph shows that her original complement of five 4.7in guns has been reduced to one in 'B' position and one in 'X' ('A' position now has a 'Hedgehog'); her funnel aft has been reduced in height, and note also her depth charge throwers at the stern and her AA guns.

8,9. The first three *Scott*s, *Scott* herself, *Bruce* and *Douglas*, were laid down in December 1916, and the others, *Campbell, Malcolm, Mackay, Stuart* and *Montrose*, in April 1917. At the outbreak of war in 1939 *Bruce* was considered ineffective and placed on the disposal list; *Stuart* had long been transferred to the Royal Australian Navy and the remaining ships were converted into escort destroyers. *Scott* herself had been torpedoed by a U-boat in August 1918. Both photographs show *Campbell* during June 1942. Note that 'X' gun has been removed: with wartime modifications such as radar it produced too much topweight, and over 50 tons of ballast had to be placed in the hold as compensation and to provide stability.

▲10 ▼11

10. *Malcolm* in her role as an escort destroyer, seen here making her way to Algiers Harbour in 1942 with US troops on board. Note that her mainmast, along with her radar aerials, have been completely removed from the photograph by the wartime censor: when such an erasure affects the negative, the view of the ship is spoilt forever. The ship's depth charge equipment is clearly seen at the stern, as is the after 4.7in shield and gun.

11. During the spring of 1916 it became necessary to counter new German destroyer designs with a more powerful type than the 'R' Class, and in order to commission a group of 28 boats with the least delay it was decided to adopt the previous design, with limited modifications. On completion, the vessels were probably the finest and most efficient destroyers then in existence, and the unqualified success of the design meant that it formed the basis for further First World War types in the Royal Navy (and was also widely copied abroad). *Viscount*, seen in the photograph, was typical of the 'V' Class, and is shown here in August 1942 after her conversion to a long-range anti-submarine escort. Note the Type 286PQ general warning radar fitted at the head of the foremast and that 'A' and 'Y' 4in guns have been removed.

12. *Vega* was one of the destroyers to be converted into an anti-aircraft escort. The modifications were carried out at Devonport from September to October 1939, after which the ship worked up at Portland before joining the Rosyth Escort Force. It will be noticed that the armament has been modified to four 4in guns in twin mountings and that 0.5in AA guns have been added *en echelon*, port and starboard, before and abaft the searchlight platform. The original superstructure has been replaced with new, heavier bridge-work. The photograph was taken late in 1942.

13. Except for triple instead of twin torpedo tubes, and a tall mainmast to accommodate Poulson W/T, the 'W' Class were repeats of the 'Vs'. The photograph shows *Winchester* steaming at 25kts on 5 July 1942, after her conversion to an anti-aircraft escort destroyer. Note the large rangefinder on top of the bridgework, used to direct the newly fitted twin 4in dual-purpose guns; no radar for the guns has yet been fitted, although it was probably added at a later date. Note also the two four-barrelled 0.5in machine gun mountings between the funnel and the searchlight platform: the original mainmast has been removed to give better arcs of fire for these weapons.

▲14

14. The 'W' Class destroyer *Wolfhound* shows off her improved features after conversion to an anti-aircraft escort destroyer: the new slimline, one-piece bridgework forward; the support legs to the foremast; the absence of her 4in guns from 'A' and 'Y' position; and her new 0.5in mountings in front of her 44in searchlight. The photograph is dated April 1943, and the lack of camouflage is interesting – by this time nearly all vessels of this type were wearing either Admiralty Disruptive or Admiralty Intermediate camouflage. During her conversion to an AA ship in 1941, *Wolfhound* was fitted with experimental Denny Brown stabilizers – the first ship of her type to be fitted with this equipment.

15. A good broadside view of the 'W' Class destroyer *Watchman* after conversion to an anti-submarine escort and showing her wartime additions. Note that the forefunnel has been removed, as has the 'A' position 4in gun (replaced by a 'Hedgehog' anti-submarine mortar). Depth charge throwers and racks have been fitted at the stern, together with radar installations Types GW 291 and SW 271Q and AF/DF MF/DF aerials at the head of the vertical pole aft. The gun armament comprises four 4in and four 20mm.

16. *Whitehall* was one of the fourteen Admiralty-modified 'Ws' and differed from the first group of 'V&Ws' in having 4.7in instead of 4in guns and two 2pdrs instead of one 3in gun. These destroyers were the last group designed for the Royal Navy during the 1914–18 war period but were completed too late for service in that conflict; however, *Whitehall* (and most of the other 'V&Ws') served in the Second World War, and was converted into a long-range anti-submarine escort in 1942–43. During the Dunkirk campaign she brought out 2,250 men; she patrolled the Western Approaches for most of 1941; she was on Gibraltar convoy duty in 1943, assisting in sinking *U306* in the North Atlantic; and she helped sink both *U314* and *U394* whilst in the Arctic in 1944. The photograph shows her in 1943.

17. A starboard bow view of *Verity*, a modified 'V' Class destroyer, in 1943. The modified bridgework is topped with radar Type 271Q, and 'A' 4.7in gun has been taken out and replaced by a 'Hedgehog'. The ramp above the A/S mortar served as blast shield. Other armament comprised two 4.7in guns ('B' and 'X' positions), one 12pdr, and four to six 20mm AA.

▼15

16▲ 17▼

▲18 ▼19

18. A view of *Vimy*, showing clearly the layout of her decks after conversion to an anti-submarine escort. The forward funnel has been removed, together with the boilers serving that uptake – a move seen as necessary in order to accommodate the additional fuel required for the ship's duties as a long-range escort. This arrangement applied only to the Atlantic escorts because the AA conversions were intended primarily for coastal escort work where a large radius of action was not mandatory, and these destroyers retained three boilers and two funnels. The photograph shows *Vimy* in November 1942, shortly after her conversion.

19. A destroyer design proposed in February 1917 resulted in the laying down of 33 vessels based on a modified 'R' type, and then a further 34 vessels two months later: Known as the 'S' class, or 'modified *Trenchant*s', they were slightly faster in service than the 'V&Ws' but had one less 4in gun. *Sabre* is here shown at anchor on 25 November 1944 whilst being used as an experimental ship for testing the latest acoustic torpedo equipment.

20. An aerial view of *Scimitar*, showing the layout of an 'S' Class destroyer, 1942. The depth charge equipment is spread over the whole length of the quarterdeck.

21. Destroyer construction ceased after the First World War and was not recommenced until the Admiralty asked several specialist firms to submit designs for a suitable vessel which would embody all wartime experience. Thornycroft and Yarrow were two of the companies invited, and both submitted acceptable designs, *Amazon* and *Ambuscade* respectively. The ships represented an improvement over a modified 'V&W', with provision for a speed increase of up to 3kts. Both saw service during the Second World War, often being used to test new equipment. *Amazon*, shown here in 1943, was used as a 'flying target training ship' during 1944; she was finally scrapped in 1948, her companion following her the next year.

22. The 'A' class were a development of the experimental *Amazon* and *Ambuscade*. *Active*, launched in 1929, appears here in 1944, following her conversion to an anti-submarine escort, with 4.7in guns in 'A' and 'X' positions only. She is also equipped with two parachute and cable projectors and two 6pdrs.

20 ▲

21 ▲   22 ▼

▲ 23

23. In August 1941 *Achates* was unfortunate enough to run on to a mine, which blew off the entire bows of the vessel, including 'A' gun and its shield. The destroyer did not, however, sink, and was towed back to the UK, stern first, for repairs. She was back in service by mid-1942 but was lost during the Battle of the Barents Sea in December that year when she was hit by 8in shells from the German heavy cruiser *Admiral Hipper* whilst trying to protect a Russian convoy.

24. The 'B' Class were closely similar to the 'A' Class with only small modifications. *Boadicea*, built by Hawthorn Leslie and launched in 1930, retained her 'A' position 4.7in gun; her sisters *Beagle*, *Basilisk*, *Blanche*, *Brazen* and *Bulldog* all had their 'A' gun and mounting replaced by a 'Hedgehog', although *Brilliant* and *Boreas* also kept their three 4.7in weapons. *Boadicea* was converted

to an AA escort 1942–43.

25. *Bulldog* was one of the old 'B' Class destroyers; unlike many of her sisters, including the leader *Keith*, she survived the war. Note that the 'A' gun position has been replaced by an anti-submarine (A/S) mortar and that the rangefinder has been removed from the bridge, RDF Type 273 having been fitted in its place.

26. *Decoy* was one of nine ships forming the 'D' class, and was laid down under the 1930 Estimates. The design was a 'B' type with very few modifications, and, except for slight differences in depth charge and torpedo tube fit, the equipment was identical. The photograph shows *Decoy* passing the battleships *Malaya* and *Queen Elizabeth* in 1941. Six of the class had been lost by the end of 1941, and it was decided to assign *Decoy* to Royal Canadian Navy along with the previously transferred 'C' Class destroyers.

▼ 24

25▲   26▼

▲27

▲28 ▼29

27,28,29. *Defender* was bombed and badly damaged by Italian aircraft off Tobruk on 11 July 1941, and, after an unsuccessful attempt by the 'V' class destroyer *Vampire* to take her in tow, she was abandoned. This series of photographs shows her settling by the stern, her back apparently broken. She went down the next day.

30. The 1931 Estimates provided for eight destroyers and one leader. All the class saw action during the Second World War, and the first taste came for *Eclipse* in April 1940 when she was hit by a bomb and damaged so badly that she was later abandoned; she did not sink, however, and was towed into Lerwick after surviving almost six days at sea in heavy weather. Repaired, she joined the Fleet once more and was involved in many sorties until sunk by a mine off Kalimine in the Dodecanese on 24 October 1943.

31. *Faulknor* was the leader of the 'F' Class and slightly larger than her sister-ships. The 'E' and 'F' Class leaders (*Exmouth* in the 'E' Class) marked the return of the policy to build leaders slightly larger and heavier than their contemporary destroyer groups, a practice which had been temporarily discontinued after the *Codrington* Admiralty leader of 1930 had been completed. *Faulknor* was laid down in May 1933 and began her sea trials in September 1934, commissioning as the leader of the 5th DF, Home Fleet, in November 1934. She was scrapped in 1946. The photograph was taken in 1942.

▲32 ▼33

32. *Fame*, an 'F' Class destroyer, photographed in 1943 and showing RDF Type 271 above the bridge, a 'Hedgehog' (covered) in 'A' position and HF/DF aerials on the vertical pole aft. Note the single-mounted 0.5in machine guns abreast the bridgework. *Fame* survived the war was latterly used as an anti-submarine training ship before being sold to the Dominican Navy in 1948.

33. *Glowworm* was probably the most famous of the 'G' Class destroyers, thanks to her most gallant action against the German heavy cruiser *Admiral Hipper* on 8 April 1940. She had become detached from the main force whilst searching for a man overboard and the cruiser opened fire with 8in guns, quickly scoring hits on the vulnerable British vessel. However, in the tradition of heroism in the Royal Navy, *Glowworm*'s commander put up a smokescreen and turned on a course for collision: although *Hipper* tried to blow the destroyer out of the water, and finally tried to avoid her,

Glowworm struck the cruiser's side and made a large gash in the plating, badly damaging the larger ship. The gallant destroyer, by now well ablaze, slipped beneath the waves leaving only 40 survivors.

34. *Gallant*, a 'G' Class destroyer launched in 1935, was one of a class of nine which included the leader *Grenville*. The whole class saw extensive action during the Second World War, six of the class being sunk. *Gallant* herself struck a mine in the Mediterranean on 10 January 1941 but did not sink: she was towed over 100 miles to Malta, where she was docked, but during an air attack on 21 January 1941 she was badly damaged by bombs and had to be beached, as shown in the photograph.

35. *Garland* served with the Polish Navy, being handed over in May 1940. She is seen here sporting Admiral Disruptive camouflage and fitted with the usual RDF and DF aerials.

▲ 36

▲ 37

36. With very little modification, the 'H' (or *Hero*) Class repeated the design of the 'G' group. *Havock*, having been in commission for only two years when the Second World War broke out, was one of the units involved in the First Battle of Narvik on 10 April 1940. Together with *Hardy* (leader), *Hunter*, *Hostile*, and *Hotspur*, she steamed into Ofotfjord, Norway, through raging snowstorms, sank two German destroyers and badly mauled three others; the British warships also completely wrecked 25 merchant vessels. *Hardy* and *Hunter* were lost in the action, whilst *Hotspur* and *Hostile* were seriously damaged. *Havock* met her end two years later when, as the photograph shows, she grounded off Tunisia on 6 April 1942; stuck fast and abandoned, she became a total loss.
37. *Hotspur* in 1945, wearing Admiralty Standard camouflage. After an extremely busy war she was sold to the Dominican Navy.
38. *Hasty*, an 'H' Class destroyer, seen at full speed in the Mediterranean in 1941–42. The ship was sunk by aircraft on 15 June 1942.
39. *Inglefield*, a member of the *Icarus* Class, was the last British destroyer to be rated as a leader. She was one of nine ships provided under the 1935 Estimates in which quintuple torpedo tubes were introduced for the first time. She commissioned at Devonport on 25 June 1937 as leader of the 3rd DF in the Mediterranean Fleet, in which position she served until October 1939. The photograph shows her entering Malta Harbour during this period and wearing Spanish Civil War recognition bands on the gun shield. She took part in the invasion of Sicily from July to September 1943, providing fire support, and in the Anzio operations from January to February 1944. It was during these latter actions that *Inglefield* was struck by a German glider bomb and sunk with a loss of 37 men.
40. The destroyer *Icarus* in October 1942, before her conversion to an escort ship. She retains her four 4.7in guns ('A' gun was removed in 1944) and has limited RDF installations.

▼ 38

▲41

41. Designed as a reply to the large Italian scout destroyers commissioned in 1928–29 and to German boats laid down in 1934–35 to which British contemporaries were obviously inferior, the *Tribal* Class combined offensive power, speed, and seakeeping qualities to an extent never before equalled in British destroyers. They were designed mainly for breaking up enemy flotillas by gun action, this aspect of the armament being emphasized at the expense of numbers of torpedo tubes. In the photograph *Ashanti* shows off her Admiralty First Disruptive camouflage. Note the tripod forward, the four twin 4in guns (which could be elevated or depressed as a single unit) and RDF Types 285 and 286M.

42. The first group of *Tribals* was ordered in March 1936 and completed in 1938–39; the second group was ordered in June 1936 and completed around the same period as the first group. The class comprised a total of sixteen destroyers, *Afridi*, *Somali*, *Cossack* and *Tartar* being fitted as leaders (although they were not classed as such). *Bedouin* took part in the Second Battle of Narvik in April 1940 and was lucky to survive a torpedo attack by *U25*. Later, whilst serving with the Mediterranean Fleet and escorting a Malta convoy, she was attacked and disabled by Italian cruisers. She was taken in tow by *Partridge*, but the tow had to be abandoned owing to the presence of enemy warships. Left to her fate, she was later attacked by enemy aircraft and hit by a torpedo. She sank on 15 June 1942.

43. Twelve *Tribals* were lost during the war but *Eskimo* survived to be scrapped in 1949. She is seen here, in April 1944, with her newly fitted lattice mast. RDF Type 286PQ was replaced by GW 291 and 293 (seen at the top of the mast) and the ship was also equipped with Type 242 IFF. Note the prominent rangefinder at back of bridge and the aerial for RDF Type 284 which controlled the main guns; others of the class were fitted with Type 285 for this purpose.

44. One of four surviving *Tribals* at the war's end, *Tartar* saw extensive action and earned herself twelve battle honours during the conflict. She took part in the *Bismarck* chase in May 1941; she escorted Russian convoys in 1942; she was present during the North African invasion in November 1942; she saw action with German E-boats off Bone on 29 April 1943; and she took part in the invasion of Sicily and Italy from June to September 1943. The photograph shows her in 1944 with all her war modifications, including lattice mast, RDF, MF/DF and disruptive camouflage.

▼42

43▲   44▼

▲45

▲46   ▼47

45. Twenty-two boats of the 'J', 'K' and 'N' Classes were provided under the 1936 estimates. The initial design was prepared after a full discussion with experienced officers from the fleet destroyers had taken place, and the ships were somewhat smaller than the *Tribal*s. Admiralty requirements called for a suitably powerful armament, two sets of torpedo tubes and minesweeping gear, and the most obvious characteristics were a very low profile and a single funnel instead of two. *Jervis*, *Kelly* and *Napier* were fitted as leaders, and *Napier*, *Nepal*, *Nestor*, *Nizam* and *Norman* were all transferred to the Royal Australian Navy on completion in 1941. *Jackal* (shown) was lost after she had been hit and disabled by a German dive-bomber off Crete on 13 May 1942: taken in tow by *Jervis* she was later abandoned and sunk by torpedo.
46. *Jupiter* early in 1942, shortly after she had sunk the Japanese submarine *I160* on 17 January 1942. She served with the Eastern Forces from 25 February 1942, and was in action with a Japanese

squadron on 27 February 1942 when she was sunk, some reports suggesting that she hit a mine.
47. *Javelin* in July 1944, showing her newly fitted lattice mast, improved RDF and Admiralty Standard camouflage. Her armament for this period comprised six 4.7in guns, four 2pdrs, four 40mm AA, six 20mm AA, ten 21in torpedo tubes and two depth-charge throwers. Note the RDF Type 293 at the head of the lattice mast. *Javelin* was present at the Battle of Matapan in 1941 and at the Normandy landings in 1944. She was sold in June 1949.
48. *Jervis* in 1942, with tripod foremast and lacking radar. The ship took part in the Battle of Matapan on 28 March 1941, firing a torpedo at the heavy cruiser *Pola* as the Italian vessel lay stricken following her engagement with the battleships *Barham*, *Warspite* and *Valiant*, and putting two torpedoes into *Zara* to finish her off. *Jervis* received thirteen battle honours, a total equalled only by the destroyer *Nubian* and surpassed only by the battleship *Warspite*.

49. A superb port bow view of *Jervis* at the end of the war. She is
sporting Pacific camouflage – light grey with a light blue hull panel.
Note the extensive RDF array.

▲50 ▼51

30

50,51. *Kelly* was one of
the most famous
destroyers of the Second
World War and will be
remembered as the ship
in which Lord
Mountbatten served.
Built by Hawthorn
Leslie on the Tyne, she
was completed for
service on 23 August
1939 and joined the
Home Fleet. Amongst
her many exploits, she
was torpedoed and very
badly damaged whilst in
action with German E-
boats on 9 May 1940.
Towed to the Tyne by
Bulldog with her upper
deck almost awash (as
seen in the photo-
graphs), she was
rammed *en route* by
another E-boat; the
latter sank, but *Kelly*
managed to reach port.
Whilst serving in the
Mediterranean in the
spring of 1941, she was
bombed and heavily
damaged: she capsized,
floated bottom up for
about half an hour and
then sank.
52. *Kimberley* survived a
torpedo attack off
Tobruk on 12 January
1942 when she had her
stem blown off, and did
not see action again until
the Southern France
landings in August 1944.
Here, Prime Minister
Winston Churchill is
seen with members of
the crew whilst watching
these landings.
53. *Kipling* in action
during the Second Battle
of Sirte, 22 March 1942,
when a force of ten
British destroyers and
four light cruisers
stopped a considerably
stronger enemy (which
included the battleship
Littorio) from sinking a
convoy bound for Malta.
Kipling survived the
battle only to be sunk by
aerial bombing two
months later, on 11
May.

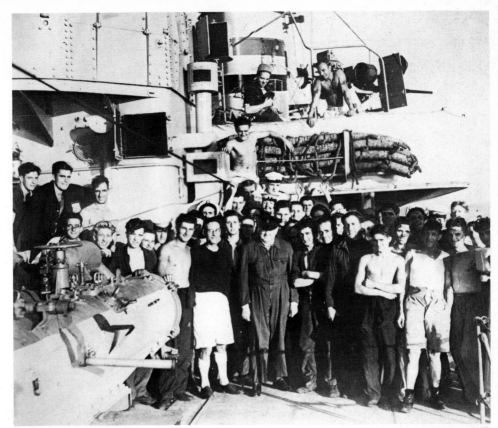

52▲   53▼

▲54

54. After being damaged by a 15in shell from an Italian battleship during the action off Sirte on 22 March 1942, *Kingston* managed to reach Malta where she docked for repair, as seen in this photograph. She was subjected to aerial bombing whilst in dock and was badly damaged, and six days later, on 11 April, during a further raid on the docks by German dive-bombers, she was hit again and capsized, breaking her back and becoming a total loss.

55. *Napier* in the Indian Ocean, early 1942. This destroyer served with the Eastern Fleet from February 1942 until late 1945, although she was temporarily attached to the Mediterranean Fleet from May to June 1942 for the Malta convoys. She took part in the operations against Sabang on 19 April 1944 and was present at the Barosa landings in December 1944. She attended the Japanese surrender in Tokyo Bay on 27 August 1945. She was not scrapped until 1956.

▼55

▼56

56. *Nizam* (seen here serving with the Eastern Fleet, 23 December 1942) was built by John Brown, Clydebank, and loaned to the Royal Australian Navy on completion. She was present at the evacuation of Tobruk from August to October 1941 and assisted the operations against Okinawa from March to May 1945. She also was present at the Japanese surrender in Tokyo Bay. The ship was broken up at Grays, Essex, from 1955.

57. *Nestor* was another 'N' Class destroyer loaned to the Royal Australian Navy. Her wartime career included the sinking of the German submarine *U127* off Cape St. Vincent on 15 December 1941. Whilst on Malta convoy to Alexandria she was attacked by German aircraft and badly damaged by near-misses (see photograph); a tow by *Javelin* was abandoned and *Nestor* was scuttled on 16 June 1942, the day after the attack.

58. The 'L' Class were slightly enlarged and modified editions of the 'Js', with a similar hull but with extra beam and 160 tons heavier. *Loyal*, seen here on 30 October 1942, shows the mid-war modifications typical of the class: note the Type 242 IFF at the foremast top, the Type 285 radar on the gun director, the single 20mm AA gun abreast the bridgework and the pom-pom behind the funnel. *Lookout* and *Loyal* were the only surviving units of the class by March 1944.

▲59

▲60 ▼61

59. *Legion* participated in the Battle of Sirte on 22 April 1942 when a Malta convoy was attacked by Italian heavy ships. She was not badly damaged during this engagement but on 23 April she was subjected to aerial attack and almost disabled by near-misses. With her engine room damaged and partly flooded, she was towed to Malta and beached. On 25 April 1942 she was again bombed, this time sinking as a result of direct hits.

60. *Lance* photographed in Malta after an aerial attack on 5 April 1942. She was hit by two bombs in the first attack, and then sustained one near-miss which blew in the side of the ship and knocked the vessel off her blocks during a second attack. A third attack wrecked part of the upperworks aft and the destroyer was proclaimed to be a total loss. She was refloated in June 1943 and towed to the UK, arriving at the Thomas Ward Shipbreaking works in Essex to be scrapped in June 1944.

61. *Laforey*, leader of the 'L' Class, was attached to the Mediterranean Fleet from August 1941 until March 1944, one of her many operations being the rescue of survivors from the sunken aircraft carrier *Eagle* on 12 August 1942. In action against *U223* off Palermo, *Laforey* forced the submarine to surface but received a torpedo hit from her foe and sank, leaving only some 60 survivors.

62. *Matchless* was another of the seven vessels of the 'M' Class laid down under the 1939 programme and built to Admiralty design. The ship is pictured on 10 August 1943 leaving the UK for duties on the Malta and Russian convoys. On 26 December 1943 *Matchless* took part in the destruction of the German battlecruiser *Scharnhorst*. She was sold to Turkey in August 1957 and renamed *Kilicali-Pasha*.

62▶

▼63 ▲64

65▶

63. The 'M' Class were modified editions of the original *Laforey* design with six guns in closed turrets instead of eight in open shields. *Martin* is depicted, off the North African coast during the landings there. The destroyer was struck by a U-boat torpedo off Bougie on 10 November 1942 and sank, taking with her approximately 150 of the crew.

64. *Meteor* showing all her twin 4.7in guns at maximum elevation. The single 3in gun amidships replaced the after torpedo tubes, and four 2pdr quadruple mountings were fitted abaft the funnel and four 20mm AA singles to port and starboard abreast the bridge. The

ship assisted in the sinking of *U314* in the Arctic on 30 January 1944, and it is recorded that *Meteor* was the last British destroyer in action in the Mediterranean theatre. She was sold to Turkey on 16 August 1957 and renamed *Piyale-Pasha*.

65. *Marne* photographed off Gibraltar after being damaged by *U515* on 12 November 1942; note the extensive disruption abaft 'X' mounting. Joining the Home Fleet, 3rd Flotilla, in April 1944, *Marne* was engaged in Russian convoy duty from October of that year and in April 1945 supported the landings in Italy in company with *Lookout*. The vessel was sold to Turkey in August 1957.

▲ 66

66. *Hesperus* was one of six destroyers to the general design of the British 'H' Class laid down for Brazil in 1938 by private yards in the UK and purchased for the Royal Navy on the outbreak of war under the 1939 Emergency Programme. She was completed by Thornycroft on 21 January 1940 and joined the Scapa Defence DF. She sank a total of five U-boats: during the encounter with *U357* on 15 January 1942 she damaged her bows, as shown in the photograph.

67. A photograph of *Hesperus* as she appeared in 1944.

68. The 'O' Class were the first destroyers built under the War Construction Programme, and were reduced (and cheaper) editions of the 'J' and 'M' groups. In order to expedite delivery, the class were armed with such guns and mountings as were readily available: *Offa, Onslaught, Onslow* and *Oribi* had four 4.7in for their main armament whilst *Obdurate, Opportune, Pathfinder, Orwell, Penn, Petard, Obedient, Pakenham, Paladin, Panther* and *Partridge* were each given three 4in. This is *Offa*, in 1941, whilst serving with the Home Fleet.

▲ 67   ▼ 68

69. The 'O' and 'P' Classes were often criticized for being undergunned, but it was stressed that they possessed the ability to fight their armament in almost any weather and were excellent seaboats – comments which would not apply to all destroyers. The 4in guns were given an extremely high angle of elevation (almost 80 degrees), reportedly to enable them to deal with German Focke-Wulf Fw 200 long-range reconnaissance aircraft. *Opportune* is seen here in 1943; the radar suite has been deleted by the censor.

70. The 'O' and 'P' Class vessels were generally similar in appearance to the 'J' and 'M' groups but could be distinguished by their smaller gunshields enclosing single rather than twin mountings. This typical wartime photograph shows *Orwell* on 11 May 1943 while serving in the North Atlantic.

71. *Obdurate* on 26 August 1942. Note the RDF Type 285 on the gun director and GW 286M at the masthead, the 44in searchlight, the 2pdr quadruple mounting behind the funnel and the single 3in gun aft. The ship served on the Russian convoys during December 1942 and saw action with the German heavy cruiser *Admiral Hipper*. She was later damaged by an acoustic torpedo. She was used for explosives tests from 1959 to 1964 while based at Rosyth.

69▲

H.M.S. "ORWELL" 11·5·43

70▲ 71▼

▲72

72. The designed shaft horsepower for the 'Os' and 'Ps' was 4,000, for a speed of 34kts, but the latter could be reached only when the vessels were in normal load conditions – at deep load displacement only 31kts could be achieved. The 'O' to 'Z' groups differed from prewar boats in having only two boiler rooms, serving one uptake, instead of three rooms serving two. This is *Penn*, in March 1942.

73. During 1943–44 the single 44in searchlight amidships was removed from *Pathfinder* and Type 271Q surface warning radar was fitted in its place; other RDF installations at the time were Type 285 (main armament) and GW Type 291. Fits differed from ship to ship within the 'O' and 'P' group, but all were fitted with MF/DF (although not all had the tall vertical pole aft to accommodate the aerial).

▼73

74. A very clear photograph of *Petard*, taken on 16 March 1945 and showing her Pacific camouflage. Improvements evident since completion in 1942 are the new lattice mast and RDF Type 293, whilst the original main armament of three 4in guns in single mountings has been replaced by four 4in in twin mountings. The 3in single gun has also been removed and four 20mm AA added in its place. *Petard* was converted into an anti-submarine frigate in 1952–53.

75. The 'Q' Class destroyers were slightly enlarged editions of the 'Os' and 'Ps', with small variations in detail – they were approximately 165 tons heavier, 14ft longer and 9in beamier and had an extra 6in of draught. All were armed with four 4.7 Mk. IX guns, four 2pdrs, six 20mm guns and eight 21in torpedo tubes. They could be identified from the 'O' and 'P' Classes by the shape of their gunshields and the separate director and rangefinder on top of the bridge. This view shows *Quickmatch* in 1943.

▲76

▲77　▼78

76. *Queenborough* on 6 December 1942, shortly after completion. The illustration shows well the general layout of these ships: 'A' and 'B' 4.7in guns; the bridge with MF/DF on the face and the rangefinder with RDF Type 285 for the 4.7 guns at the rear; the tripod foremast; the raked funnel; the quadruple 2pdr mounting; the forward quadruple 21in torpedo tubes; the 44in searchlight platform with 20mm AA guns in front; the after quadruple torpedo tubes; 'X' and 'Y' guns; and the depth charge throwers at the extreme stern.

77. *Quail* as completed, 1942. Of the 'Q' Class, *Quiberon* and *Quick-match* were loaned to the Royal Australian Navy in 1943, with *Quadrant*, *Quality* and *Queen-borough* following in 1945; *Quail* and *Quentin* were war losses. Except for *Quilliam*, all the surviving ships were permanently transferred as a gift to the Royal Australian Navy in June 1950 on condition that they were converted into anti-submarine frigates; *Quilliam* was sold to the Netherlands in 1945. *Quail* hit a mine on 15 November 1943, and although an attempt to tow her to Bari proved successful, she foundered whilst being taken from Bari to Taranto, on 18 June 1944.

78. *Quality* at anchor in Devonport in 1942. Only RDF Types 285 and 290 are fitted at this time, Types 272 (lantern) and 242 being installed on the searchlight platform later in 1943. The pennant number G62 is shown, but when some of the group served in the Pacific with the United States Navy they were temporarily given 'D' numbers, *Quality* being D18.

79. The initial design for the eight 'R' Class destroyers was proposed in November 1940 and virtually matched the 'Q' Class, although a modified accommodation plan was featured. As completed, these destroyers were extremely difficult to distinguish from the 'Q' Class, but they carried power-operated twin instead of manually worked single 20mm AA guns abreast the bridge.

80. The 'R' Class were the first British destroyers to have officers' accommodation forward, a modification introduced as a result of war experience in the North Atlantic when it was frequently found impossible to relieve officers of the watch and after gun crews owing to heavy seas flooding the upper deck amidships. *Rapid*, built by Cammell Laird, is seen here in the River Mersey just prior to her deployment to the Eastern Fleet on a commission which lasted until October 1945.

81. *Roebuck* in the summer of 1943, showing the newly fitted RDF Type 272 on a small lattice tower over the searchlight platform. US-pattern Type SG surface warning radar was also fitted, low on the foremast. On 12 March 1944 *Roebuck* caught the tanker *Brake* off Mauritius and sank her while the German ship was trying to refuel two U-boats. All the 'R' Class destroyers were converted into A/S frigates after the war.

79▲

80▲ 81▼

▲82

▲83   ▼84

85▲

86▲

82. As leader of six 'S' class destroyers, *Saumarez* certainly saw plenty of action during the Second World War. One of her first tasks was to escort the liner *Queen Mary* carrying Prime Minister Churchill to Canada in August 1943, and on 26 December that year she took part in the destruction of the German battlecruiser *Scharnhorst* off the North Cape, hitting her with two torpedoes. In the Far East, the 26th Flotilla, of which *Saumarez* was leader, attacked and sank the Japanese heavy cruiser *Haguro* in the Malacca Straits on 15 May 1945. On 22 October 1946 the destroyer hit a mine in the Corfu Channel; she was taken in tow by *Voltage* to Malta but was not considered worth repairing and the hulk was finally sold on 8 September 1950. The photograph shows *Saumarez* on 7 October 1943.

83. The 'S' group were slightly larger than the 'R' Class, and together with the later 'T' to 'Z' Classes were officially known as a 'utility' type in which essential war requirements took precedence over all other considerations. The boats were not expected to last for more than five years in continual service and their finish was stated to be below the standard required for peacetime construction, many fittings considered necessary in the 'Js' being omitted. *Swift* is illustrated, on 8 December 1943 whilst serving with the Home Fleet; on 24 June 1944 she struck a mine off Normandy and sank, with 55 casualties.

84. In August 1943 the decision was taken to fit the first two 4.5in Mk. VI mountings to one of the 1943 *Battle* Class destroyers. Prototype weapons were installed in *Savage* as one twin turret forward and two singles in shields aft. The rest of the 'S' Class were fitted with four 4.7in Mk. IX guns. *Savage* was used for gunnery experiments and for propeller and shaft tests after the war and was sold for scrapping in 1962. This photograph of her was taken in May 1943.

85. The 1940 Programme provided for eight 'T' Class boats, which were closely similar to the 'S' group; they were built to an Admiralty design produced by Stanley Goodall. The main armament, four 4.7in, and the two 40mm AA were controlled by RDF – Type 285 for the 4.7s and Type 282 for the AA weapons. *Tumult* is seen here early in 1944, with Mount Vesuvius in the background. As completed, the ship was temporarily fitted with experimental torpedo tubes, fixed to port and starboard amidships and angled slightly outwards; her normal equipment was restored at the end of 1943.

86. *Termagant*, built by Denny and completed on 18 October 1943 (when this photograph was taken), went straight to the Mediterranean as part of the 24th Destroyer Flotilla. She assisted in the sinking of *U453* off Spartivento on 21 May 1944, and in October that year, in company with her sister *Terpsichore*, she attacked and destroyed five ex-Italian torpedo-boat destroyers in the Aegean. The flotilla transferred to the Pacific late in 1944 and *Termagant* was present at the Japanese surrender in Tokyo Bay. She was placed in reserve in 1947.

▲87

▲88 ▼89

87. *Terpsichore* (shown, January 1944), *Teazer, Tenacious* and *Termagant* were completed with a heavy lattice mast but the others of the group were given light tripods; a vertical lattice pole was placed aft for the HF/DF or RDF in *Teazer, Troubridge* and *Tyrian*. All these destroyers were converted into anti-submarine frigates from 1951 to 1957.

88. *Grenville* was the leader of the 'U' Class, which comprised eight vessels; provided under the 1941 Programme, she was completed in 1943. The general design features of the 'S' Class were perpetuated, *Grenville* being fitted with a light tripod foremast and her sister-ships with heavy lattice foremasts to provide adequate support for the ever-increasing RDF installations. By mid-1943 *Grenville*'s RDF aerials consisted of GW 291 at the head of the foremast, Type 285 for main armament control and Type 282 for the 40mm AA, but the equipment has been censored in this March 1944 view.

89. Another view of *Grenville*, in 1943, showing the RDF installations and the MF/DF on pole aft.

90. *Ursa* on 4 February 1944, as completed and showing Admiralty Standard camouflage. The 'U' Class proved to be very good seaboats and could be driven hard without becoming unduly wet. Note the HF/DF aerials at the top of foremast; these were later removed and replaced with RDF Type 291.

91. A port bow view of *Ursa* taken at the same time as the previous photograph.

90▼

91▼

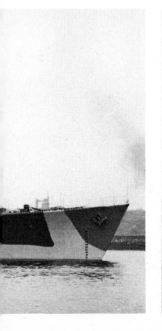

▲92

▲93 ▼94

95▲

92. *Hardy* was the leader of the six 'V' Class destroyers, the sister-ships being *Venus*, *Verulam*, *Vigilant*, *Virago* and *Volage*; a further two boats built to the same design, *Valentine* and *Vixen*, were transferred the Royal Canadian Navy on completion and renamed *Algonquin* and *Sioux* respectively. She was built by John Brown and completed in 1943 for service with the Home Fleet, but the following year, whilst escorting a Russian convoy off Bear Island on 30 January, she was torpedoed by a U-boat and mortally crippled. Attempts to save her proved to be in vain, and she was abandoned and sunk by her companions. The photograph was taken in 1943; note the stump mainmast, and also the lattice pole aft topped with HF/DF.

93. The 'V' Class were repeats of the 'S' to 'U' group, and were designed by Goodall under the 1941 Programme. The leader *Hardy* was the only war loss, and the others saw plenty of action from 1943 to 1945. *Vigilant* took part in the destruction of the heavy cruiser *Haguro* on 15 May 1945, hitting the Japanese ship with one torpedo. She is shown on here 4 September 1943, as completed by Swan Hunter. Note the RDF Type 276 at the masthead and Type 285 on the gun director; Types 242, 272 and 291 aerials are also visible.

94. A port bow view of *Verulam* taken on 8 December 1943, just two days before she was commissioned. Note the flat-faced turrets which house the 4.7in Mk. IX guns, and the director (with Type 285 radar) which controls these turrets. The 44in searchlight behind the funnel was later removed. One particular feature of these destroyers was the spraying of the deckheads with asbestos to insulate the living spaces from the extreme cold. The class were all converted to anti-submarine frigates from 1952 to 1955.

95. The eight 'W' Class destroyers, led by *Kempenfelt*, were provided under the 1941 Programme, were repeats of the 'S' to 'V' ships and formed yet another group within the 'utility' classes. *Whirlwind*, shown, was completed in July 1944 and joined the Eastern Fleet as part of the 27th DF. She took part in the bombardment of Sakashima Island in May 1945, surviving attacks from kamikaze aircraft during this operation.

96. *Wager* on 5 May 1944, as completed for service. Note the heavy LA/HA director, with rangefinder incorporated, on top of the bridge. The 'Ws' were the last British torpedo boat destroyers to feature a 4.7in LA armament and were also the first complete destroyer class in the Royal Navy to be fitted with a heavy lattice foremast. *Wager* was sold to Yugoslavia and renamed *Pula* in 1957.

97. *Kempenfelt* on 4 August 1944. As leader of the 'W' class, she was some 20 tons heavier than the rest of the flotilla but was otherwise identical. After the war she was sold to Yugoslavia and renamed *Kotar*.

96▼

97▼

▲98 ▼99

98. *Wrangler* served in the Pacific during the war and was present at the Japanese surrender in Tokyo Bay on 28 August 1945. Postwar she was employed as a boys' training ship until her conversion to an anti-submarine frigate by Harland and Wolff from June 1951.

99. *Zest* was the last of the 48 almost identical 'S' to 'Z' Class 'utility' destroyers built in six groups and completed from 1943 to 1944. The 'Z' group differed from the others in having a 4.5in dual-purpose main armament instead of 4.7in guns. Note also the heavier gun director of this class (reported to be Mk. III) and the large screens placed around the 40mm AA mountings. The photograph was taken on 12 December 1944, a few months after the destroyer commissioned.

100. A February 1945 photograph of *Zebra*. Permanent fore and aft bridges over the torpedo tubes were introduced in this class in place of the light wire catwalks of the earlier boats.

100 ▼

▲101 ▼102

101. *Zambesi* as she appeared in 1944: note the RDF Types 285, 293, 282, 291 and 242 IFF. This vessel took part in the evacuation of civilians from Soray Island off the Norwegian coast on 15 February 1945. Postwar, she was used as an anti-submarine target and tender from May 1951 to June 1952 and was placed on the disposal list in the summer of 1958.

102. Numerically, the largest destroyer class built for the Royal Navy since the 30-knotters of 1897 were the eight 'CAs', eight 'CHs', eight 'COs' and four 'CRs'. There were originally to have been four flotillas each of eight boats, but four of the 'CR' group were never commissioned in the Royal Navy: *Crescent* and *Crusader* were loaned to the Royal Canadian Navy on completion in 1945, and *Cromwell* and *Crown* were sold to Norway whilst under construction. Although the 'CA' group were practically identical to the 'Z' Class, the others differed in having improved gunnery equipment, a reduced torpedo armament and part of their construction electrically welded. This is *Cavendish*, in February 1945.

103. Of these groups, only the eight 'CAs', *Chevron* and *Comet* were completed before the end of the war, and these vessels served with the Home Fleet. *Crispin* ('CR' group) is officially stated to have been the first all-welded destroyer built for the Royal Navy. This photograph of *Cambrian* taken in October 1944 shows well the deck layout of the class.

104. The 'C' groups were the last British destroyers to have a main armament in single mountings and in open shields. *Carron* was built by Scotts of Greenock and completed in November 1944, serving with the 6th DF in the East Indies until the summer of 1946. She was laid up in 1963.

▲105 ▼106

105. The *Battle* Class destroyers were designed with a view to Pacific operations, and embodied many lessons arising from war experience. There were sixteen boats, all designed by Goodall for the 1942 Programme. They were 650 tons heavier than the 'C' groups, were about 1–2kts slower and had their main armament concentrated forward. *Armada,* *Barfleur* (shown), *Camperdown* and *Trafalgar* were the only units of the class to see service before the war ended.

106. It was originally proposed to use 'A' and 'B' names for the *Battle* Class vessels, but when it was found that they would be constantly compared with the *Tribals* it was felt that a more distinctive set of names should be chosen. This is *Trafalgar*, on 3 October 1945; note the RDF Type 275 on the main director.

107. In August 1938 Admiral A. B. Cunningham (then about to take up his appointment as Deputy Chief of the Naval Staff) was approached by the First Sea Lord for his opinions as to the best means of rectifying the serious shortage of destroyers. Cunningham, who had previously been impressed with the qualities of the 1918 'S' Class, suggested a small vessel along these lines. The result was the *Hunt* Class, and to facilitate the passage of such a large programme through Parliament the first twenty vessels were referred to as 'fast escort vessels'. They were intended mainly to replace the larger fleet destroyers on escort work for short ocean and coastal convoys. *Cotswold* is illustrated, in 1941.

▲108 ▼109

110▲

108,109. A total of 86 *Hunt* Class vessels was built, in four groups distinguished by variations in dimensions and armament. The original 1939 design provided for six 4in dual-purpose guns and some light AA, but the first boat completed, *Atherstone*, was found deficient in stability and two 4in weapons, together with other weights, were removed from the Type Is to remedy this. The Type IIs, however, had increased beam for better stability, and it was found possible to carry the full suite of six guns. The Type IIIs had their armament reduced to four 4in guns, and the pair of Type IVs,

built to a Thornycroft design, featured a heavier armament and a reduced speed. The photographs show *Hambledon* (Type I) in October 1942.
110. *Berkeley* (*Hunt* Type I) was seriously damaged when attacked by aircraft during the Dieppe raid on 19 August 1942, receiving several very near misses which blew in her side plating. The photograph shows her settling down and listing to starboard. She was later abandoned.
111. The *Hunt* Type I destroyer *Pytchley* off Sheerness in 1943.

111▼

▲112 ▼113

112. *Quantock*, another *Hunt* Type I, was built by Scotts of
Greenock and completed for service in the autumn of 1940. She
accounted for a Dornier bomber in the North Sea in November
1941 and was present at the Salerno and Sicily landings in
September 1943. She was sold to Ecuador in 1954 and renamed
Presidente Alfaro.
113. A view of *Puckeridge*, a Type II *Hunt*, showing the forward
twin 4in dual-purpose guns, the RDF Type 285 on the director,
IFF Type 242 and HF/DF aerials. The 2pdr anti-E-boat bow-
chaser was not commonly featured in Type II *Hunt*s.
114. *Cottesmore* photographed during the 1944 Normandy landings.
This Type I was sold to Egypt in 1950 and renamed *Mohamed-Ali*.

115. *Eridge* (Type II) was built by Swan Hunter on the Tyne and
completed in 1941, joining the Mediterranean Fleet in March 1942.
She was attacked and damaged by an E-boat in August 1942; towed
to Alexandria (as seen in the photograph), she was subsequently
employed as a base accommodation ship. She was sold in 1946.
116. *Calpe* was a Type II *Hunt*, built by Swan Hunter and
completed in 1942. The modification needed to increase the stability
of these vessels was effected whilst the boats were on the stocks by
means of adding an extra strake of plating at each side of the keel –
simple but effective! As completed, these destroyers were, for their
size, very good seaboats, and they stood up to severe weather
conditions exceptionally well.

▲117 ▼118

119▲

117. Since they were intended mainly for escort duties and anti-submarine work, the *Hunts* were given an adequate sea radius, and the Type IIs had a maximum fuel capacity 65 tons greater than their predecessors. They could stay at sea for seven or eight days under normal war conditions – although for a very much shorter period if a considerable amount of fast steaming was called for.

118. *Glaisdale* (*Hunt* Type III) in June 1942.
119. Only two units of the *Hunt* Type IV group, *Brissenden* and *Brecon*, were completed; they were slightly larger than the vessels of the other three groups and *Brissenden* shows here how the forecastle deck extended well aft before dropping to form the quarterdeck. The photograph is dated 10 February 1943.

▲120 ▼121

122▲

120. In 1940 the United States supplied the Royal Navy with fifty destroyers which had been built at the end of the First World War. All were renamed, after towns and villages common to both countries. The vessels were used mainly for escort duties, and gave a much needed boost to the RN during a period when it was pushed to the limit. *Ripley* (ex-*Shubrick*) is shown.
121. Another view of *Ripley*. Note the depth charges on the stern, the torpedo tubes, the RDF lantern (Type 273) on top of the bridge, the differing heights of the funnels and the sharply inclining deck lines.
122. *Lincoln* (ex-*Yarnall*), was built by William Cramp and Son and completed in 1918. The illustration shows the destroyer in 1942 and gives a clear idea of the layout of these vessels.

▲123

123. A photograph of *Clare* (ex-*Abel P. Upshur*), built by Newport News and completed in 1920.

124. The ex-American destroyers suffered heavily during the war and about half of them were either lost or damaged beyond repair. *Beverley* (ex-*Branch*), seen here in 1942, was torpedoed by a U-boat off Greenland on 10 April 1943.

▼124